Wrest Park

Andrew Hann and Shelley Garland

CONTENTS

Tour of the House   3

Exterior and Setting   3
Morning Room and
Adjoining Rooms   4
Countess's Sitting Room   4
Conservatory   5
Entrance Hall   6
Staircase Hall   6
Ante-library   8
Drawing Room   8
Library and Print Room   8
Dining Room   10
Service Wing and Stables   12

Tour of the Gardens   14

Development   14
Walled Garden   18
Italian Garden   18
Rose Garden   19
Terrace and Parterre   20
Round Pond and Site
of Old House   21
Orangery   23
Bath House   24
Evergreen Garden   24
Bowling Green House   25
The Great Garden   26
Dairy   35
Petit Trianon   35

History   37

Special Features

Thomas, Earl de Grey,
the Architect   11
The Wallpapers of
Wrest Park   13
The Old House at Wrest   22
Thomas Archer   29
The Evolution of the
English Garden   32
The De Grey Mausoleum   44
De Grey Family Tree   46
Wrest Park Hospital   48

Plans

Plan of the Gardens   16
Site plan   inside back cover

Tour of the House

The house at Wrest is the remarkable creation of one man, Thomas, Earl de Grey, who built it between 1834 and 1839. When his aunt died and left him Wrest Park in 1833, de Grey inherited an outstanding garden with a crumbling house of medieval origins. Rather than improving the old house, de Grey demolished it and built a magnificent new one some 200m to the north.

EXTERIOR AND SETTING

The house and gardens were once surrounded by parkland (now returned to agricultural use). The river Hit, which runs to the south, feeds the canals and water features in the gardens. The approach to the old house was from the north, but de Grey designed his new house with a western approach from the village of Silsoe, through an impressive new gateway flanked by lodges de Grey had designed himself in 1826, before he inherited the estate, in his first use of the French style.

The approach took visitors along a tree-lined avenue and past the expanse of de Grey's new walled garden (see page 18) with the ornate Eagle Gate at its centre (now the main visitor entrance): it was clearly designed to be admired before the imposing north front of the house came into view.

De Grey was a gifted amateur architect and designed a number of buildings, but Wrest was the only one where he employed the French style. It was an unusual choice at a time when Italianate and Gothic styles were more common, and was probably driven by a desire to tie the gardens, which were in part influenced by French fashions, and house together stylistically (see page 11). The foundation stone (visible in the conservatory), was laid on 12 February 1834 and the family moved into the house in the autumn of 1839.

Above: De Grey's creation, Wrest house, from the north. 'He wished to create the château of a French Grand Seigneur', wrote a family friend, Ralph Sneyd, in 1855
Below: Anne, Lady Cowper (see page 47), her daughter Amabel and grandson Ralph, on the drive north of the house, late 19th century

Right: Convalescent soldiers relaxing in the billiard room in December 1915, when Wrest Park was in use as a military hospital during the First World War

Below right: The Countess's Sitting Room, also known as the Boudoir, in about 1865. The five small paintings over the door are portraits of the children of the 6th Earl Cowper, painted by Frederic (later Lord) Leighton when he visited Wrest in 1861

1 MORNING ROOM AND ADJOINING ROOMS

The suite of rooms at the west end of the house, through which visitors now enter, originally comprised a sitting room, bedroom and dressing room, probably for Mary, de Grey's second daughter. By 1846 the bedroom in the centre had been made into a sitting room, and the dressing room beyond it into a billiard room. Today they contain exhibitions on the development of Wrest Park and the people who lived and worked here.

2 COUNTESS'S SITTING ROOM

De Grey created this room for his wife, Henrietta, or Nett, as she was known by those closest to her, with the intention that 'no lady sets foot in it without thinking that the man who invented such a jewel of a place must be "a sweet man"'; by his own account he was much satisfied with the room. Like the other ground-floor rooms, it is in the French style, but decorated with a lighter touch. De Grey noted that the doors and window shutters were salvaged from France and intended for Windsor Castle, but never used there. He bought them from a London dealer, using them as the starting point for the room.

Although de Grey reused little from the old house at Wrest, the cupids in the ceiling decoration come from its library and the fireplace from its south drawing room. On the velvet panels on either side of the fireplace, and elsewhere in this intimate room, were displayed portrait miniatures of family, friends and famous figures. On either side of the conservatory door hung portraits of four of Henrietta's five children (only three lived to adulthood and only her eldest two daughters outlived her). The room is today furnished to reflect how it may have looked in

'Lady Grey … is clad in white flowing muslin and she sits in a room of white satin and gold and china and miniatures' Cecilia Parke describing Henrietta, Countess de Grey (above, as Psyche, by Sir Thomas Lawrence, 1814), in September 1839

3 CONSERVATORY

This light, airy room with elaborate iron-framed roof and windows was, unusually for the time, designed to be an integral part of the house. It was paired with the dining room at the opposite end of the garden front to retain the overall symmetry of the design.

The sets of doors leading from the Countess's Sitting Room and out to the gardens are aligned to allow a clear view through the conservatory to the Italian Garden and walled garden beyond. From here the countess could monitor the activities of her household. As de Grey described it, the conservatory 'opens out of her sittingroom, all the doors and gates from her fireplace to the furthest extremity of the kitchen-garden are so disposed that she can see the whole length and inspect every dung barrow that is wheeled in at Snow's [the head gardener's] house'.

The bronze trellis is original, as are the slate-edged planters at the base of the walls (those in the centre are new, replacing 20th-century concrete versions). These are now planted to the original scheme although, as the conservatory is no longer heated, hardier modern varieties of plants have been chosen.

the 1840s, including some surviving pieces of furniture, such as the pair of giltwood cabinets on stands to either side of the entrance. The chintz chair covers match the pattern shown in a photograph of the room from about 1865.

Above: The restored conservatory, planted with hardy plant varieties capable of withstanding the cold (the room is no longer heated)
Above left: The Countess's Sitting Room refurnished to reflect how it would have looked in the 1840s. Surviving furniture includes the overmantel mirror, seen here, and a pair of giltwood cabinets on stands
Left: An early colour photograph of the Italian Garden and conservatory by a local photographer, T W Latchmore, in about 1930

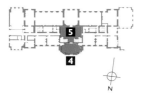

Right: The entrance hall with its wainscot panelling and playful frieze of frolicking putti
Below: View from the entrance hall through the building and garden to the pavilion at the head of the Long Water. De Grey designed the house with this magnificent vista in mind

4 ENTRANCE HALL

The elegant oval entrance hall has central doors opening onto the staircase hall beyond, and smaller doorways on each side which led to de Grey's suite of offices on the left and the billiard room on the right. The American birch panelling was inspired by some that he had admired in a house he rented in 1830 in Hastings and which he copied in 1833 when making alterations to his family's London house, 4 St James's Square. Above the panelling is a high frieze depicting groups of putti, or cherubs, made of carton-pierre (a kind of papier mâché using stone dust instead of paper). The marble floor incorporates the earl's coronet and was constructed by a local stone mason.

5 STAIRCASE HALL

Through the central doors is the magnificent staircase hall, originally used to hold receptions. It reaches the full height of the building and is capped with a glazed oblong roof, a lantern, that allowed light to flood the space below. De Grey initially intended a gallery to run around the upper floor, with rooms opening from it, but decided against this when he realized that 'Every housemaid in clearing out the rooms hears every thing said below; and every gentleman who lounges below sees every housemaid, both very objectionable.'

From here the twin branches of the staircase draw the eye upwards to the portraits of family and royalty assembled here from several of de Grey's houses. The staircase handrail is of an unknown wood from South America given to him when he was First Lord of the Admiralty in the mid 1830s by Lord William Fitzroy. Once a purple and silver colour, it has dimmed over the years. The frames of the portraits were made to form part of the decoration of the hall, the designs taken from de Grey's books of French architecture depicted in the frieze above the ante-library door. The names of the 17th- and 18th-century French architects Blondel, Mansart and Le Pautre are carved on the spines (see page 11).

Flanking the doorway to the ante-library are statues by the contemporary neoclassical sculptor Richard Wyatt of Rome depicting Hebe and a bathing nymph. The brass grilles in the floor are hot air outlets for the heating system, one of the earliest in England, which was supplied by a coal-burning boiler in the basement.

Left: The staircase hall (c.1844) by Thomas Scandrett. The chairs against the walls were bought after being used at a dinner, probably in Dover, for the Duke of Wellington in the 1830s; the chair in which he sat was marked with a 'W'. The portraits show (from left of entrance)

Queen Anne, by Godfrey Kneller

Queen Caroline, wife of George II, by Jacopo Amigoni

Amabel, sister of Henry, Duke of Kent, by John Clostermans

Philip, 1st Earl of Hardwicke, Lord Chancellor, father-in-law of Jemima, Marchioness Grey, by William Hoare

A **Sophia Bentinck,** second wife of Henry, Duke of Kent, by Amigoni

B **Henry Grey, Duke of Kent,** by Kneller

C **Jemima Crew,** first wife of Henry, Duke of Kent, with her daughter Jemima, by Kneller

D **Amabel Grey, Lady Glenorchy,** eldest daughter of Henry, Duke of Kent, by Jacques d'Agar

John, Lord Somers, Lord Chancellor, by Simon Dubois

Jemima Grey, Lady Ashburnham, daughter of Henry, Duke of Kent, by Charles Jervas

Anne, Princess Royal, wife of the Prince of Orange, by Amigoni

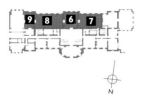

6 ANTE-LIBRARY

This room was intended as a billiard room, a fashionable addition to country houses at the time, but the plan was abandoned as it would have impeded the main view south into the garden from the staircase hall. It was decided instead that it should serve as an addition to the library.

The finely carved cornice below the ceiling includes emblems representing war, peace and history, to reflect some of the subjects of de Grey's book collection. The corner fireplace is in the French rococo style and is probably one of a number that de Grey bought in bulk from a sales house in Paris. In the opposite corner is a carved and gilded outlet for the original hot air heating system. Today a radiator is concealed within it.

7 DRAWING ROOM

The drawing room is at the west end of the suite of formal rooms forming an enfilade (each room opening onto the next) along the length of the garden front of the house. Initially de Grey had no intention of having a drawing room, considering them outmoded and expecting his family to use the library as a sitting room, but concern that critics might think the omission an error led him to include one in the end. The family did not use

Top right: The painting on the ceiling of the drawing room by John Wood. De Grey commissioned him to create something with 'pretty faces and gay colours'

Right: One of four paintings on the library ceiling representing Music, Painting, Poetry and Sculpture, by John Wood. Here 'Sculpture' leans on the bust of de Grey

Below: Anne Florence, the dowager Lady Cowper (right), and her daughter Amabel Frederica in the library in about 1865

the room often, reserving it for balls and other formal events that de Grey, as Lord Lieutenant of Bedfordshire, was obliged to host.

The blue wallpaper is a 20th-century addition, a replacement for the tapestries from the French workshop in Beauvais that de Grey commissioned for the room. They were sold, as were most of the contents of the house, in 1917. De Grey commissioned the painting on the ceiling from the relatively little known John Wood RA, whom he described as 'a very good artist in the pretty face line'. The room was originally illuminated by large glass chandeliers.

8 LIBRARY AND 9 PRINT ROOM

The library was in a sense the heart of the house, both the room in which the family spent most of their time and that which determined the proportions of the rest of the house. De Grey considered it early on in his designs, intending from the start a 50ft (15m) room, with a pair of fine French fireplaces. The bookcases and carved

Above: *Thomas Scandrett's watercolour of the drawing room in about 1844, showing the full effect of the striking Beauvais tapestries that de Grey commissioned for the room (they were sold in 1917)*

Left: *Florence Amabel Cowper (left) and her sister Amabel Frederica, daughters of the dowager Lady Cowper, with one of their dogs, Dandie, in the drawing room in about 1865. The crystal chandeliers were the only ones in the house; by the 1830s de Grey considered them unfashionable, although appropriate for this room*

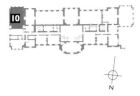

the cornice were painted by de Grey himself and represent the arms of the various families related to the de Greys by marriage.

The print room was intended simply as a corridor between the library and dining room, but soon became used for books and prints as the family's collection expanded.

10 DINING ROOM

Although still predominantly French in style, like the rest of the house, the dining room brings together a number of other influences. Its unusual plan – it narrows at each end – is copied from the dining room de Grey designed in 1808 for his Yorkshire house, Newby Hall. He found such an arrangement 'convenient and agreeable as it allowed for larger dinners or smaller gatherings'.

The fireplace came from de Grey's London house, which he inherited at the same time as Wrest, and the designs of the pilasters and ceiling were taken from the old house at Wrest, the ceiling being copied from the old library, with the addition of heraldic emblems, a theme de Grey used throughout his new house.

The four elaborately modelled trophies on the cornice – possibly by Joseph Bass, who executed much of the plasterwork at Wrest – represent

scroll work panelling were bought at auction, as were a pair of carved oak picture frames used as door-heads here and in the ante-library.

The four allegorical panels depicting music, poetry, painting and sculpture are by John Wood. The one closest to the windows includes a portrait bust of de Grey upon which the muse of sculpture leans. The armorial motifs in the escutcheons on

Above: A daughter of the Duke of Kent standing beside an orange tree, perhaps from the estate orangery. This portrait, by an unknown artist of the English school, now hangs in the library

Above right: The sons of the 2nd Lord Grantham, by Sir Joshua Reynolds: Thomas (1781–1859), Frederick (1782–1859) and Philip (1783–94). Thomas went on to build the new house at Wrest. The painting used to hang in the dining room, to the left of the door, as can just be seen in the watercolour on the right

Right: Watercolour view of the dining room in about 1844 by Thomas Scandrett

Thomas, Earl de Grey, the Architect

Thomas, Earl de Grey, was, as his father before him, an amateur architect. Of the various works completed by the end of his life, Wrest, the only example of his use of the French style, is perhaps his greatest legacy. There is little architecture in England in the 18th-century French style: perhaps the best known is Waddesdon Manor in Buckinghamshire, built in 1874 for Baron Ferdinand de Rothschild, 35 years after Wrest was completed. Usually, English architects borrowed only details, decorating interiors in the French fashion. But at Wrest de Grey employed the French style throughout.

Influences

De Grey travelled extensively in Europe in his youth and wrote in his memoir of his admiration for buildings he saw in Paris. In creating Wrest de Grey relied heavily on a trio of books on French architecture bought in Paris, probably books by the three French architects whose names are shown on the spines of the three books depicted above the door to the ante-library at Wrest: Jacques-François Blondel, François Mansart and Antoine Le Pautre.

De Grey's first use of the French style was in the lodges at Wrest flanking the Silsoe gate in 1826 – by which time he was already forming ideas for the main house: 'they looked so well and appropriate when finished that I felt quite confirmed as to the taste and the style of architecture, if ever I built a new house.'

The entrance front at Wrest is reminiscent of the work of one of Mansart's collaborators, Louis Le Vau, at the famous 17th-century chateau Vaux-le-Vicomte in Maincy. As de Grey himself recalled: 'I had my French books always under my hand!' But despite being, as he wrote to his daughter Anne in 1846, 'strictly and in every sense of the word my own architect', de Grey needed assistance: 'there were things respecting which I frankly acknowledged my utter ignorance, *viz*, prices of materials, value of men's wages, custom of trade and business and so forth'. He hired as his clerk of works James Clephane, a London architect and builder recently employed in a similar role by Lord Barrington, who had built Beckett Park in Berkshire.

Work Beyond Wrest

De Grey's architectural work included public buildings, such as Ripon gaol, the redesign of the interior of his London house on St James's Square, and works for which he gave his expertise as part of a committee, as in the extension of Buckingham Palace and completion of the new Houses of Parliament. In 1826 he refused to allow John Nash to reuse a staircase from Carlton House in the United Services Club, deeming it too narrow, and his own designs were used instead. In 1835, while at work on Wrest, de Grey was elected first president of the (later Royal) Institute of British Architects, a post he held until his death in 1859.

'I was as you know strictly and in every sense of the word my own architect'

Above: Drawing by Earl de Grey of the north elevation of his new house at Wrest in the 1830s
Left: Portrait of Thomas Philip, 3rd Lord Grantham, afterwards 2nd Earl de Grey, by Sir Thomas Lawrence, about 1814
Below: View into the garden from the staircase hall, showing the bas relief that includes de Grey's three 'French books'

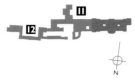

Right: Detail of the trophy depicting 'flesh' on the south wall of the dining room. It was for this that de Grey had the head of a local pig brought to Wrest to inspire the craftsman

Below: Hetty Geyton (right), the cook, and her kitchen staff in 1916. During the First World War the kitchen provided meals for some 200 convalescing soldiers and nurses

fish, flesh, fruit and fowl. De Grey recalled: 'the modelling of these subjects was very good fun. We had a large basket of every sort of fish from London, and arranged them on a large slate table in the most picturesque attitudes. We were rather at a loss for a boar's head, but a reference to some German books on sports, and an actual head of an enormous real hog which was killed in the village that week, enabled us to surmount our difficulties.'

After the death of his wife in 1848 de Grey became increasingly involved with the lives of his two surviving adult daughters, Anne and Mary, who spent long periods at Wrest. To amuse them and his grandchildren, he put on a number of theatrical performances, often written and acted by family members. It was at this time that de Grey had the rear wall of the dining room modified. Wheels and pulleys allowed it to be moved back to form a stage and a trap-door enabled the actors to rise up out of the floor. Although the moving wall is no longer operational the mechanism remains, hidden above the ceiling.

Paintings by Sir Joshua Reynolds originally hung on either side of the door, one of Amabel, Countess de Grey, and her sister Mary Robinson, and the other of Mary's three boys, Thomas, Frederick and Philip. Thomas, the eldest, later became Earl de Grey and builder of the new house at Wrest.

⓫ SERVICE WING AND ⓬ STABLES

The large service wing to the east of the house was built by de Grey at the same time as the rest of the house and is one of the earliest examples of a specialized service wing in the country. It housed the kitchens, larders, sculleries and laundries needed for the smooth running of the household.

Connected to the main house by corridors running the length of the basement, the service wing has three staircases which gave the servants access to the upper floors of the main house. At the far end are the stables, where horses and coaches were kept.

The Wallpapers of Wrest Park

Since the late 1930s most of the rooms on the upper floors have been used as offices. Few original features remain, but judicious boarding over in the 1940s protected rare wallpaper in three rooms.

The Chinese Wallpaper

The paper in the Chinese bedroom and dressing room at the top of the stairs is 18th century and probably once hung in the old house at Wrest: Amabel, daughter of Jemima, Marchioness Grey, refers in her diary to her mother's buying and hanging such wallpaper in 1792.

These hand-painted Chinese papers were vastly expensive and considered the height of luxury. They first arrived in Europe in the late 17th century and peaked in popularity between about 1740 and 1790 during the craze for oriental goods that followed the rise of colonial power in the East.

The paper is painted with landscapes, figures and birds. Repetition of details on a later European paper between the windows, above the fireplace and on the section of wall that would once have been hidden by the bed, suggest that additions had to be made when this valuable paper was moved from the old house. A four-post bedstead with cornices and silver dragons listed in a 1917 auction catalogue possibly once stood here; the mechanism for bells used to summon servants can be seen on the wall where the bed would once have stood.

The French Wallpaper

At the western end of the first floor is a room hung with scenic block-printed wallpaper by the French company Zuber, founded in 1797 at the peak of the fashion for French wallpaper and still in business today. The design, 'Eldorado', illustrating America, Asia, Europe and Africa, with accurate depictions of plants and animals, was first used in 1848 so could not have been the original decorative scheme in this room. It was probably hung when Earl de Grey's granddaughter Henrietta Vyner and her cousin Viscount Goderich used rooms at this end of the house for their honeymoon in 1851.

Complex and expensive to make, French scenic wallpaper was a luxurious product, and is rare in Britain. 'Eldorado' was made using 1,554 different blocks and 120 colours; the example at Wrest is the only known complete set in the country.

Complex and expensive to make, French scenic wallpaper was a luxurious product

Above: Scene representing Europe from the 19th-century French wallpaper, 'Eldorado'
Below: A detail of the 18th-century wallpaper from the Chinese bedroom

Tour of the Gardens

INTRODUCTION

The gardens at Wrest form one of the most complete remaining early 18th-century formal landscapes in the country, with additions that mark every major development in English garden design until the mid 19th century. Wrest also has a number of important 18th- and 19th-century garden buildings, including Thomas Archer's magnificent baroque pavilion, and a nationally important collection of garden statuary.

From the terrace the superb view south encompasses Earl de Grey's parterre of the 1830s, glimpses through the trees beyond of the encircling canals of 1758 to 1760, and in the distance the Long Water of the 1680s, inspired by the great formal gardens of France. The Long Water still defines the axis of the garden, with the ordered woodland stands of the Duke of Kent's early 18th-century Great Garden on either side.

Although never regarded as the height of fashion, the gardens were widely admired throughout their history and much visited. Many leading 18th-century garden designers and architects worked here, including Thomas Ackres, Batty Langley, Thomas Archer, Thomas Wright and Lancelot 'Capability' Brown.

In 1658 formal gardens at Wrest were noted as 'new', the work of Amabel, wife of Henry, 10th Earl of Kent. In the 1670s she and her son Anthony, the 11th earl, and his wife, Mary, expanded the gardens, and in the 1680s dug the Long Water, which formed the basis for the rest of the garden design. But it was the woodland garden, the Great Garden, created by Anthony and Mary's son, Henry, Duke of Kent, in the early 18th century that became the presiding influence over all later work.

In 1758 'Capability' Brown, a leader of the new English landscape style of the time, was brought in by Jemima, Marchioness Grey, to soften the edges of the garden and remodel the park. His influence can be seen in the sinuous canals that form an artificial river around the Great Garden and in the irregular clumps of trees that replaced many of the formal avenues. But he was given limited freedom, and the duke's gardens were only partly altered. Brown himself realized that to do more 'might unravel the Mystery of the Gardens'.

The formal flower gardens to the south and west represent the last major development, when Earl de Grey demolished the old house and built the current one further north in the 1830s, allowing space for extending the gardens.

Below: Possible design drawing of the early 1830s for the new house, gardens and park at Wrest. The plan pre-dates the building of the orangery, which replaced the green house (seen here at the bottom left). It also shows the Italian Garden extending as far south as the French parterre

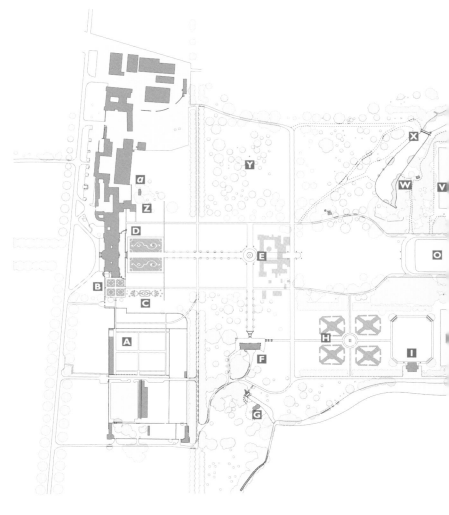

PLAN OF THE GARDENS

In 2011 English Heritage embarked on a 20-year programme to restore the gardens at Wrest, beginning with the replanting of the rose garden and Italian Garden. The main garden features are identified in the accompanying plan, although the Great Garden (see page 26) is still best explored, as in the 18th century, by wandering the many rides and paths to happen upon the numerous statues and views among the trees.

A Walled garden (entrance from the east)

B Italian Garden

C Rose garden

D Terrace and French parterre

E Round pond and site of old house

F Orangery

G Bath house

H Evergreen Garden

I Bowling Green House

J Leg o' Mutton Lake and amphitheatre

K Duchess's Square and West Half House

L Hutton monument

M Mithraic altar

N William III statue

O The Long Water

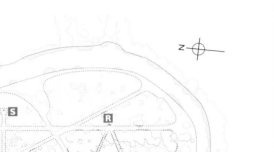

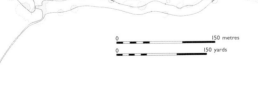

0   150 metres

0   150 yards

P Pavilion
Q Duke's Square
R East Half House
S Dogs' cemetery
T 'Capability' Brown column
U Graeco-Roman altars
V Ladies' Lake
W Chinese temple
X Chinese bridge
Y Atlas Pond
Z Dairy
a Petit Trianon

Above right: Strangers' Gate Walk, looking west, with the south wall of the walled garden on the right, 1904

Below: The Italian Garden looking west, restored to its early 20th-century planting scheme

13 WALLED GARDEN

The vast walled garden, covering an area of 6 acres (2.4ha), is divided into six compartments and was built at the same time as the house. Until the 1930s it supplied the household with a great variety of fruit, vegetables and flowers. The walls were once lined with espalier fruit trees, including peach, nectarine, pear, apricot, plum and cherry, and a number of lead plant labels are still in place, probably dating from the 19th century. In 1900 there were 21 glasshouses, including three peach houses, five vineries and a melon pit. Today only a small section of the fig house remains.

Immediately to the left of the Eagle Gate, now the main visitor entrance, are the visitor centre, café and children's play area. Beyond this is the pear orchard; where possible historical varieties of pear have been replanted in their original positions, following recent volunteer research. The wisteria around the northern wall is supported by chains attached to the walls. Although still magnificent, it is much reduced in size, having once been reputed to be the largest chained wisteria in the country. When Wrest was the base for the Silsoe Institute, from 1948 to 2006, the walled garden was used for agricultural experiments. Most of the more modern buildings within the garden date from this period.

14 ITALIAN GARDEN

This sheltered flower garden, restored to its original planting scheme, was laid out by Earl de Grey for his wife, Henrietta, and can be viewed through the conservatory from her sitting room. The colourful mix of bulbs and annuals produces a

mass of colour through much of the year. Four statues of cherubs holding fruit or flowers once stood at the angles of the walks, but only a statue by the north wall of Pomona, the Roman goddess of fruit, now remains.

15 ROSE GARDEN

The rose garden probably dates from the late 19th century when such gardens were popular. Following archaeological investigation it has been restored to its appearance in 1917. At its centre is a 19th-century Carrara marble fountain base of four mermaids supporting a (probably not original) vase. The base was probably introduced to the gardens by Anne Florence Cowper in the 1860s. The flower-beds are arranged symmetrically around it, each ending in a fan shape.

Above: The statue of Pomona in the Italian Garden
Left: The statue of four mermaids of Carrara marble, the centrepiece of the restored rose garden. Lady Anne Cowper, Earl de Grey's eldest daughter, probably bought the statue for the gardens in the 1860s

16 TERRACE AND FRENCH PARTERRE

Earl de Grey planned his 'French Garden' to complement the new house and the Duke of Kent's Great Garden beyond. Although he considered it 'original and novel', the intricate design is typical of the formal flower gardens that had become fashionable again in the early 19th century. The beds are laid out in a scroll pattern, edged with box and planted with bulbs and bedding plants. The four large groups of sculpture are 18th-century leads by the leading English sculptor John Cheere, bought by de Grey from a London dealer. They stand in their original positions: the two nearest the house are pairs of lovers, Venus and Adonis and Atalanta and Meleager; the third is the Trojan hero Aeneas carrying his father Anchises from the ruins of Troy; and the last, loosely based on the 16th-century Italian sculptor Giambologna's well-known *Rape of the Sabine Women*, may depict the rape of Helen by Paris.

Eight further statues, of the four seasons and four elements (now at Ditchley Park, Oxfordshire), stood in the corners of the two parterre segments, and on each side of the central path was a row of Portuguese laurels in Versailles tubs. From here there is a good view of the garden front of the house, possibly inspired by a design in Jacques-François Blondel's 1737 work *Maisons de Plaisance*. The terrace railings have been repainted and regilded to match the original colour scheme. The windows had green striped blinds, with blind boxes striped to match, a style suggested to de Grey by Charles Barry, one of the architects of the Houses of Parliament and a friend of the family.

The dogs flanking the central steps were brought by de Grey from his Yorkshire house Newby Hall; they are copies of the Alcibiades Dog, a celebrated Roman antique at Duncombe Park, not far from Newby. The earl bought the urns along the terrace from dealers, adding the family crest to four of them. The French parterre has been restored to its mid 19th-century layout.

Above: The French parterre on the south side of the house

Below: View of about 1831 from the old house looking south towards the pavilion, by Earl de Grey. He noted that the sundial in the foreground was placed there by Amabel, Countess of Kent, in 1682

▣ ROUND POND AND SITE OF OLD HOUSE

Portuguese laurels, originally planted in Versailles tubs, line the path down to the site of the old house. Beyond the path stands, in its original position, a fibreglass replica of the clockmaker Henry Wynne's sundial of 1682 (the original is in the dairy sculpture gallery). The old house once stood behind it and in dry summers its foundations show up as parch marks in the lawn to the north.

The fountain of Carrara marble further north, supplied with water from a cistern on the roof of the house, was installed in the 1860s by de Grey's daughter Anne Florence Cowper. The eight mid 19th-century marble statues around it were probably bought by de Grey as copies of antique sculptures. The statues around the sundial also date from the mid 19th century, but are on earlier stone pedestals. They were moved here in 1919 by John George Murray (see page 50).

Left: Two of the female figures cut from Carrara marble below the round pond fountain, which was added to the main north–south walk by Anne Florence Cowper in the 1860s

Below: View today looking south down the Long Water towards the pavilion

Right: South-west view by John Buckler of the remains of the old house at Wrest in 1838 during demolition, with 'its cracked walls and its long passages and its windows that annually became less capable of being closely shut down', as Thomas, Earl de Grey, recalled

Below: Buckler's view of the house from the south-east in 1831, before demolition began. The bay-fronted great dining room added by Jemima in 1760 is visible on the left

The Old House at Wrest

Earl de Grey considered that the old house 'had neither antiquarian or architectural value' and had it demolished in stages between 1834 and 1840

The first mention of a house at Wrest is in 1308 when Reynold de Grey held a 'capital messuage with a dovecote, worth 4s. per annum' — probably a simple structure of hall, chamber, screens passage and kitchen. A chapel was added in 1320. The Greys became increasingly powerful during the 14th and 15th centuries, and by 1573 the house included a dining chamber, low parlour and at least nine bedrooms. Few further changes were made until 1672, when Anthony, 11th Earl of Kent, and his wife, Mary (who in 1671 had inherited the fortune of her father, Lord Lucas), undertook major work to improve the house. Surviving accounts show that the 'Chapel Chamber' and Lord Lucas's apartments were remodelled, and a classical north front costing £3,227

was added. Thomas Hooper, the estate steward, oversaw the works, though the architect is unknown. Despite these improvements, the house remained an amalgam of styles, with an irregular and inconvenient floor-plan around a courtyard. The earl's son Henry, Duke of Kent, intended to rebuild it in a classical style to the design of Italian architect Giacomo Leoni, but abandoned his plans after losses in the South Sea Bubble, the death of his two remaining sons in 1717 and 1723, and the burning down of his London house (which he had rebuilt by Edward Shepherd between 1725 and 1728). Instead, in the 1730s he had the architect and garden designer Batty Langley create a new dining room in the south-east part of the house.

Later changes were similarly piecemeal: in 1760 Jemima, Marchioness Grey, added a great dining room with a bay window to the south front and in 1791 refaced the north and south fronts and added a Chinese drawing room to the east of the servants' hall. These were the last changes made to the old house. Thomas, Earl de Grey, who considered it 'had neither antiquarian or architectural value', 'of very bad construction' and 'very extensive without possibility of concentration', had it demolished in stages between 1834 and 1840.

Left: De Grey's orangery today, from the east
Below: The orangery chimneypiece, of about 1600, from old Wrest house. It bears the de Grey coat of arms and motto 'Foy est tout' ('Faith is everything')
Bottom: Batty Langley's green house from Rocque's 1737 plan of Wrest, showing orange trees in boxes on the south terrace. The orangery replaced it in the 1830s

18 ORANGERY

The French-style orangery was built in the 1830s during the re-landscaping of the upper gardens. It replaced Batty Langley's green house of 1735–6, which had stood on the same terraced bank, but aligned east–west. De Grey based it on a design for a trianon, or grand garden pavilion, in Blondel's 1737 book, *Maisons de Plaisance*. The roof ornaments were made by artificial stone manufacturer Felix Austin.

The orangery was once stocked with French orange trees, bought from King Louis Philippe of France. By the end of the 19th century these were said to be among the largest in the country. The potted trees were wheeled out in summer through two concealed full-height doors on the right of the building, the doors to the front being too low. The presence of these high doors is revealed from the outside by little more than a pair of discreet metal runners set in the ground. As de Grey remarked: 'What a cunning arrangement I devised here – for if you look at the stonework closely, you'll see it is not a window but in fact a concealed door.' The trees were set out on the slope below, or along the path towards the fountain. Photographs of the early 20th century show this still in practice.

The pump which brought water from a tank in the basement stands next to the concealed doors inside the orangery. The elaborate chimneypiece, of about 1600, is from the old house at Wrest and was retained in the steward's room in the service wing of the new house until 1935, when it was removed elsewhere. It was returned to Wrest and the orangery by the Ministry of Works in 1954.

The Green House.

20 EVERGREEN GARDEN

The Evergreen Garden was laid out by de Grey in 1857, replacing the Duke of Kent's formal elm grove of the early 18th century. It was occasionally referred to, as early as the 1860s, as the American Garden because of its acid-loving plants commonly found in North America. Such exotic gardens became fashionable in the early 19th century as access to New World plants increased. The garden has been restored to de Grey's original design: four symmetrical oblong segments defined by two tiers of yew hedging and planted with yews, laurels and rhododendrons.

At the centre is a sculpture group known as *The Hawking Party*, made by the Irish sculptor Terence Farrell to the earl's design. It includes a statue of a horse that had been intended for the entrance to the stable block, to which was added a lady with a hawk on her wrist and a page by her side. Until 2010 *The Hawking Party* was surrounded by Blue Atlas cedars, planted in 1935, but these were removed as part of the restoration work.

19 BATH HOUSE

Surrounded by water and informal evergreen planting, the ironstone bath house is reached across a simple bridge which straddles a natural spring. This once filled the circular cold plunge pool inside the bath house and fed the network of canals in the gardens. The bath house, possibly altered by de Grey between 1813 and 1830, was designed by Edward Stevens in 1769–70 for Jemima, Marchioness Grey, and resembles a semi-ruined classical building, patched up in a rustic way, with a thatched roof and cobble floor inlaid with a pattern of deer bones.

This 'picturesque' style was part of the new English landscape gardening popular from the mid 18th century and inspired by the landscapes of artists such as Claude Lorrain, whose paintings often show Italian wildernesses populated by ruins. Its introduction at Wrest can probably be attributed to Jemima's tutor, Thomas Wright, who had interests in both garden design and antiquities. Other picturesque features such as the Mithraic Glade may have been inspired by his ideas.

Above: *The bath house today*
Right: *The Hawking Party, the centrepiece of the Evergreen Garden. A hawk once perched on the woman's outstretched arm, but went missing in the 1970s*
Below: *Postcard view of the Evergreen Garden from the north in about 1906. At the time, Wrest was leased to the American ambassador Whitelaw Reid*

Left: East view of the Bowling Green House from John Rocque's 1737 plan of Wrest. The arched yew hedge shown here surrounding the bowling green was partially cleared by Earl de Grey to improve the view from the orangery to the amphitheatre beyond
Below: The chimneypiece on the north wall of the Bowling Green House with the armorial bearings of the Duke of Kent. The interior was redecorated by Batty Langley in 1735 as part of his remodelling of the building, and restored in 2004

21 BOWLING GREEN HOUSE

The brick Bowling Green House may have been built as early as 1720–21, but was altered for the Duke of Kent in 1735 by Batty Langley, who also introduced serpentine paths into the gardens and built the first greenhouse. Langley added the loggia on the east of the building to provide a sheltered view of the bowling green. This apparently solid Tuscan structure is made of painted timber. The pair of lead vases in front was supplied to the Duke of Kent by the sculptor John van Nost the younger in 1725, and was in position here by 1735.

Langley's interior, restored in 2004, is richly decorated in the style of the leading architect of the time, William Kent, with a marble chimneypiece bearing the duke's arms and the insignia of the Order of the Garter, bestowed on him in 1713. At the north end is a small service room and to the south are two privies accessed from outside. The room was originally furnished with 16 walnut chairs and various tables, but only two marble-topped consoles remain *in situ*; and there is an exhibition on the history and restoration of the gardens.

The bowling green first appears on a plan of 1719 by Edward Lawrence. It was first enclosed by a high yew hedge in a series of arches, which was partly restored in the 1960s but removed since to open the view from the Evergreen Garden.

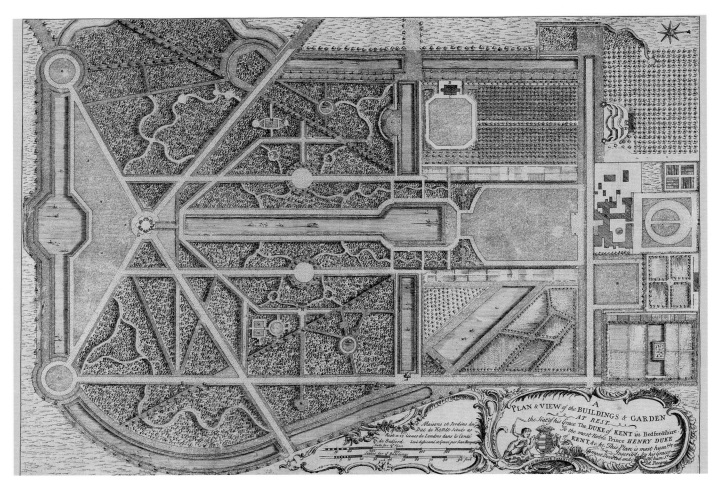

Above: Detail of John Rocque's 1737 plan of the garden at Wrest. It shows changes made to the Great Garden by Batty Langley

THE GREAT GARDEN

The Great Garden, laid out mainly between 1706 and the early 1720s for the Duke of Kent, is a rare example in England of a formal woodland garden in the French style. Although designed to make use of light, shade and the subtle hues of the greenery, rather than vivid colour, an understorey of creeping and flowering plants, including briar roses, honeysuckle and jasmine, was introduced by

'The Garden appear'd in full Beauty; the whispering of the Trees, the warbling of Birds, the surrounding Verdure, the Fragrance of Seringos and Bean Blossoms, the Gay Bloom of Roses and Honeysuckles, which are innumerable in these woods, the Smooth Canals sometimes bending like Artless Rivulets and sometimes appearing Silver Lakes with stately swans sailing up and down in them.' Jemima's friend Catherine Talbot (1721–70; left, by Christian Friedrich Zincke), writing in her diary on a visit to Wrest in June 1745

Jemima, Marchioness Grey, from the 1740s. A network of rides and paths, now with restored gravel surfaces, provide structure. Many of them were bordered by clipped evergreen hedges, some of which are being restored.

The main rides are straight and arranged symmetrically on either side of the Long Water, linked by a maze of narrow winding paths mostly introduced from the 1730s, when areas of the Great Garden were partially deformalized. The paths open onto hedged clearings populated with monuments and statues – each opening intended as a separate 'event', a surprise to be happened upon while wandering through the gardens, which remains the best way of exploring them today.

In the early 18th century the duke's gardener, John Duell, enclosed the Great Garden on three sides with formal canals fed from an existing brook and a spring in the bath house grounds. From the late 1730s the canals were shaped into the present serpentine form in phases by Batty Langley, Thomas Wright and later Lancelot 'Capability' Brown.

22 Leg o' Mutton Lake and Amphitheatre

The Leg o' Mutton Lake was formed from the western of the two east–west canals on either side of the northern, 'spade', end of the Long Water. These canals were added, probably by the Duke of Kent's gardener, John Duell, as a cross-arm inspired by the gardens at Versailles when the duke remodelled the Long Water in about 1706. The canal was originally oblong, but acquired a 'leg of mutton' shape (and its name) when the semicircular 'stage' of the earthwork amphitheatre to the south was cut away and flooded in the late 18th century. Despite its name, the lake is once again rectangular after restoration work in 1989.

23 Duchess's Square

The Duchess's Square (in fact, oval), balances the Duke's Square in the eastern half of the garden. In the early 18th century it held a brick alcove, two large pedestal urns, two busts, seats, a central column, and the lead statue of a woman reading. The column (now in Trent Park) was dedicated to the Duke of Kent's first wife, Jemima Crew, and topped by a pineapple. The statue is thought to represent Jemima, who loved to read in the gardens. It was probably installed by the duke in the 1730s. Only the alcove, known as the West Half House, and the lead statue remain.

24 Hutton Monument

This simple red-brick memorial was put up for Thomas Hutton, keeper of Somerset House, who 'took great delight' in the gardens at Wrest, by 'his Friend, Henry Duke of Kent'. Probably still on its original site, the monument was never prominent, being set into the side of one of the north–south paths through the woodland garden. It was given renewed focus in the 1740s when the Mithraic altar and root house were built nearby.

25 Mithraic Altar

Devised in 1748 by Jemima, Marchioness Grey, and her husband, Philip Yorke, this flint and stone 'altar' is an elaborate intellectual joke. As a student at Cambridge Philip and some friends wrote a volume of letters purporting to be from Cleander, a Persian ambassador to Athens in classical times, which they published privately as *Athenian Letters* in 1741 and 1743. Inscriptions on the altar in ancient Greek and Persian are inspired by these

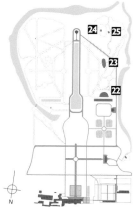

Left, top: Watercolour of the Duchess's Square by Pieter Tillemans, about 1728, showing the column dedicated to the duke's first wife, Jemima Crew

Left, second from top: Statue in the Duchess's Square of a woman reading, thought to be of Jemima Crew. It was probably erected by her husband the duke in the 1730s, though not at this exact spot, but a little south of the column shown above

Left, third from top: Watercolour of Hutton's monument from Earl de Grey's sketchbook, 'Views of Wrest', 1831

Left: The Mithraic altar, and rustic root house beyond, drawn by de Grey in about 1831. The root house was built in 1749 by Thomas Edwards, whom Jemima described as 'seated under an old oak with a table before him covered in plans and compasses ... and a whistle'

Right: The statue of William III,
by one of the brothers and
18th-century sculptors Henry
and John Cheere
Below: The Long Water in the
morning mist

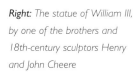

letters, and suggest it was dedicated by 'Cleander'
to the Persian sun-god Mithras. Many visitors to
Wrest were mystified by the inscriptions, much to
Jemima and Philip's amusement. Lady Anson noted
in August 1748 that the Duchess of Bedford and
her party 'took the altar for an antiquity'.

On the south side of the glade in which the
altar stands, a root house (now lost) once added
to the romantic landscape in this part of the
garden. It was designed by Philip's friend Thomas
Edwards as a dwelling for the priest of the altar
and was a basic structure of roots, billets and
moss. Jemima wrote to Philip in 1749 that it was
'happily finished, and proves very odd and pretty
whilst highly suitable to the place'.

26 William III Statue

The Duke of Kent's garden was densely populated
with statues, mainly lead figures by the leading
statuaries of the day such as the van Nost family
and Andrew Carpenter. Most were melted down
in 1809 by Philip and Jemima's impoverished
daughter, Amabel, Countess de Grey, to provide
lead for the roof of the house; among the few
survivors are the statues of the woman reading in
the Duchess's Square and of William III dressed as
a Roman emperor, by Henry or John Cheere. This
stands in its original position in front of the pavilion
on a ketton-stone pedestal with a marble plaque
celebrating the 'glorious and immortell memory' of
King William. It was installed here after 1737.

27 The Long Water

The Long Water was created before 1685 by
Amabel, known as the Good Countess, and her
son, Anthony, the 11th Earl of Kent, possibly from
earlier fishponds. It may have been modelled on
Charles II's canals of the 1660s at Hampton Court
and St James's Park. Aligned north–south, it forms
the axis of the gardens, and all later features, apart
from the bath house, were positioned with
reference to it. On either side are wide gravel
walks, recently restored, backed by laurel hedges.

28 Pavilion

Thomas Archer's pavilion, designed and built
between 1709 and 1711, provided the duke with
a pleasure house that was both a focus and a
viewing point for the gardens. It is formally
positioned at the end of the Long Water and

Thomas Archer

Thomas Archer (1668/9–1743) was an architect of independent means who held a lucrative position at court. The youngest son of a Warwickshire gentry family, he was educated at Trinity College, Oxford, from 1686 to 1689 and then travelled abroad for four years. He probably made his way to Italy via Germany and Austria and was clearly influenced by the baroque architecture he encountered on his travels, especially that of Rome. Indeed his work is more Continental than that of any other English architect of his day. He made frequent use of

eared architraves, broken pediments and unusual geometric plans with convex and concave wall planes. The pavilion at Wrest is a prime example of this delight in geometry, as was his other garden building at Wrest, Cain Hill House (demolished in the 1830s), which had an octagonal plan with alternating concave and straight sides. Of his other work, the Cascade House at Chatsworth (1702, one of his earliest commissions), St Paul's Church Deptford, St John's Smith Square and St Philip's, Birmingham, all show an idiosyncratic inventiveness.

The pavilion at Wrest is a prime example of Archer's delight in geometry

Top: Cain Hill House from the west and in plan, from John Rocque's 1735 plan of Wrest
Above: *Portrait reputed to be of Thomas Archer and attributed to Godfrey Kneller*
Left: *North view of the pavilion from Rocque's 1737 plan of Wrest*

'… *very ugly in the old fashioned manner with high hedges and canals, at the End of the principal one of which is a frightful Temple designed by Mr Archer*'
A snide description by Horace Walpole (above, by John Giles Eccardt, 1754) of the still formal gardens at Wrest in 1771, after 'Capability' Brown's restrained alterations for Jemima, Marchioness Grey

aligned directly with the centre of the house. Its six projecting bays (three round and three square) were designed to look out along six principal views radiating from the pavilion into the south end of the garden.

The pavilion was built of red and yellow brick, with rubbed brick and stone dressings. This polychromatic effect was subdued by a coat of stone-coloured render, probably applied in the 1770s. The plain plaster interior was painted by the French Huguenot artist Louis Hauduroy in 1712, with *trompe l'œil* Corinthian columns, full entablature, niches, statues and coffering. The imagery and family portraiture celebrate Henry Grey's elevation to the dukedom in 1710. Later restoration led to the loss of parts of the design.

Archer's play with contrasting geometrical forms has much in common with designs by the great Italian baroque architects Borromini and Bernini, whose work he may have seen on the Grand Tour in the 1690s, and the pavilion may be based on Michelangelo's unexecuted plan for San Giovanni dei Fiorentini in Rome. Its domed roof, cupola and Ionic portico resemble St Philip's, Birmingham (now the cathedral), which Archer also designed.

The pavilion was intended to entertain hunting parties and for occasional suppers. A 1711 plan shows how various rooms were allotted. The

central rotunda crowned by a dome rises through three floors. Four spiral staircases from the main room led to a kitchen, larder, bagnio (bath), and two-seater privy in the basement, and to what are described as servants' rooms on the upper level. The two oblong closets off the main room were furnished with a couch, chairs, cupboard and mirror, while the three semicircular alcoves each held two chairs and a table.

The inventory taken on the duke's death in 1740 recorded that in the closet to the west were 'a Red Japan Tea Table, a Teapot Stand and Slops bason [*sic*], eight large Tea Dishes & Saucers ditto, all blue and white China'. Both closets and alcoves were decorated with brightly coloured gilt-leather hangings; these were replaced with wallpaper in the 1750s when the pavilion was redecorated in Chinese style by Jemima, Marchioness Grey. Writing to her daughter Amabel in September 1761, Jemima asked her to instruct the painter to 'set about the Closets in the Pavilion, & he may begin first with the Yellow Paper, which he knows should not be deeper than straw colour, & … he must go on to the other Closet, & make that of one of these Patterns of Blue (instead of Red) whichever shade will look best with the Prints'. The current wallpaper dates from the restoration of the building in the 1950s.

The Evolution of the English Garden

The great gardens of Renaissance Italy were the foundations of the European formal garden, with its geometric layout, clipped lawns and hedges, and classical references

Above: Lady Amabel Polwarth, later Countess de Grey, in 1772, by Anne Forbes. Amabel wrote to her sister in 1778 that 'Capability' Brown thought 'a winding Water through a strait Avenue might … look inconsistent, & if the Avenue was destroy'd, & part of the Wood clear'd away, it might unravel the Mystery of the Gardens'
Right: Wrest gardens, from a view by Johannes Kip and Leonard Knyff, about 1705

To the European elite in the 17th and 18th centuries, gardens were an expression of status, learning and, often, political affiliations. Landowners such as the Duke of Kent were deeply involved in the work of their garden designers. They consulted friends and texts and drew inspiration from their experiences on the Grand Tour, where they would have seen the Boboli Gardens of the Medici family in Florence and the gardens of the Villa d'Este outside Rome. These great gardens of 15th-century Renaissance Italy were the foundations of the European formal garden, with its geometric layout, clipped lawns and hedges, and numerous classical references.

By the mid 17th century, however, France and Holland were at the forefront of garden design. The new French style was seen as a branch of architecture, even using such terms as 'rooms', 'carpets' and 'walls'. It emphasized grand vistas and geometric layout and culminated in André Le Nôtre's gardens at Versailles. Its influence can be seen at Wrest in the axial Long Water and large walled garden enclosures.

After 1702, the Duke of Kent's work on the gardens owes more to Dutch influence, which had increased after William of Orange took the English Crown in 1688. Dutch gardens were compact, with intricate ornamentation, clipped evergreens and, in England, often political symbolism to declare loyalty to William III and the Protestant succession.

By the 1730s another fashion had emerged alongside that for formal gardens – the English landscape style. Nature, rather than architecture, was the inspiration, and was recreated so expertly by gardeners such as 'Capability' Brown that the architect Sir William Chambers complained that Brown's grounds 'differ very little from common fields, so closely is nature copied in most of them'. Aware of this new fashion, Jemima, Marchioness Grey, sought to soften the edges of the gardens at Wrest from the 1740s, and to introduce greater variety through new features such as the bath house and Chinese temple. In 1758 she turned to 'Capability' Brown, but allowed few changes, wanting to preserve the spirit of the earlier gardens.

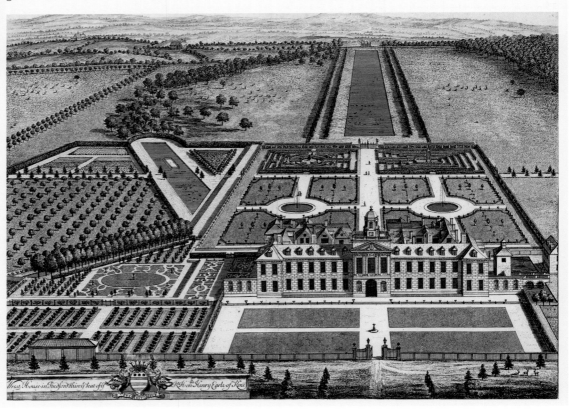

29 Duke's Square

This was created with the Duchess's Square to the west. Its linked oblong and circular compartments were originally accessed from the east, west and south. Three views of about 1726 by the Flemish painter Pieter Tillemans show the compartments bordered by clipped hedging with alcoves in which statues of cherubs stand. An obelisk dedicated to Henry, Duke of Kent, at the centre of the circular space was sold and removed to Trent Park in 1934. The oblong space held two lead urns on pedestals commemorating the duke's eldest son and eldest daughter, Anthony, Earl of Harold, and Amabel, Lady Glenorchy, both now replaced by replicas.

30 Dogs' Cemetery

This area appears on the John Rocque's 1735 plan of the gardens as a square clearing at the end of a straight path leading east off one of the Great Garden walks, the Lady Duchess's Walk. To the south along this walk is the alcove known as the East Half House, dating from the late 1720s. The dogs' cemetery dates from 1829 when Earl de Grey (then Lord Grantham) erected the Dog Monument, a statue of a dog on a stone pedestal. The 16 surviving headstones date from 1830 to 1860 and are not in their original positions.

31 'Capability' Brown Column

This column commemorates 'Capability' Brown's modification of the gardens in 1758–60 and was made for Jemima, Marchioness Grey, by Edward Stevens, who designed the bath house and bridge. It closely resembles the column formerly in the

Duchess's Square and now at Trent Park (see illustration on page 27). The addition of two rusticated blocks, however, may be one of Philip and Jemima's intellectual jokes: the blocks hinting at the 'rustication' of the gardens by Brown.

The column was moved in 1828 to its present position at the north end of the Lady Duchess's Walk from the bath house garden. Here it could be viewed by anyone crossing the canal to the south by the rope ferry that led to an alcove on the opposite bank. The ferry and alcove have now gone, but the column has been restored and the sand circle within which it stood reinstated.

Above left: Watercolour of the main circular compartment of the Duke's Square, by Pieter Tillemans, c.1728
Below left: This ketton-stone statue in the dogs' cemetery is a replica, placed on the original early 19th-century pedestal
Bottom left: The East Half House on the Lady Duchess's Walk, seen from one of the paths to the west, from Rocque's plan of 1737
Below: 'Capability' Brown column at the north end of the Lady Duchess's Walk

The Alcove Seat in the Lady Dutchess's Walk

Above: The Graeco-Roman altars in their circular grove, from Earl de Grey's sketchbook of 1831
Right: Ladies' Lake, with the statue of Diana and a greyhound by Andrew Carpenter
Below: The Chinese bridge today, spanning the canal
Below right: A view of the Chinese temple by Earl de Grey, about 1831. The young women are very probably two of his daughters, with their pet dogs

32 Graeco-Roman Altars

The five antique altars in the clearing to the west of the 'Capability' Brown column were bought and placed here by Amabel, Countess de Grey, in 1817. They stand in a circular area that has been part of the network of paths within the Great Garden since at least 1735. It was recorded as a grove in one of Earl de Grey's watercolours of about 1831 and has changed little since, apart from the loss of the central trees. The sand path has been restored.

33 Ladies' Lake

Ladies' Lake, like the Leg o' Mutton Lake, was one of two east–west canals extending at right angles from each side of the northern end of the Long Water. In the early 18th century the canals were collectively known as 'Lakes for my ladies' ducks'. They became separated from the Long Water when linking sections were filled in in about 1737. Ladies' Lake has been enclosed by yew hedging (now restored to its original position) since the mid 18th century. The statue of Diana with a greyhound by Andrew Carpenter (c.1677–1737) at the head of the lake was reinstated in 2012.

34 Chinese Temple and 35 Bridge

This area of the garden, formerly shielded from the Ladies' Lake by a high hedge, forms a separate 'set piece', reminiscent of the scenes found on Chinese tableware and wallpapers of the time. Probably created between 1758 and 1761, the ensemble included a wooden Chinese bridge, temple, conch shell water feature, willow tree and tulip tree. Only the willow tree no longer survives. The temple may have been designed by Sir William Chambers, architect of the pagoda at Kew. It was rebuilt in the 1940s and restored c.1967. The bridge has been rebuilt several times, lastly in 1876 in stone by Earl de Grey's daughter Anne Florence Cowper.

36 Atlas Pond

The statue of Atlas once stood in the centre of a circular lily pond built (probably by Lady Cowper) in the mid 19th century and now filled in. It is surrounded by the remnants of an orchard dating from the 1720s and the eastern section of the Great Yew Hedge, the western part of which edged the old green house, and was planted in the 18th century. Today the area is dominated by an enormous Giant Sequoia planted by the head gardener, Seward Snow, in 1856.

37 DAIRY

Built at the same time as the house in the 1830s, the ornamental dairy is a late example of a type of building popular in the late 18th century, when dairying was fashionable among aristocratic women. It is a free-standing pavilion, linked to the service wing of the house, with stained-glass windows, and a lattice metalwork veranda and small cupola that give it a hint of chinoiserie. It once provided butter and cream for Earl de Grey and his household.

In the 1980s the Silsoe Institute used it as part of its canteen, inserting large low-level windows (now removed). Today it displays statuary too delicate or valuable to be left out in the gardens.

38 PETIT TRIANON

Rustic log cabins such as the Petit Trianon were a fashionable feature of English gardens in the mid 19th century, the most famous example being the Swiss Cottage at Osborne House on the Isle of Wight. The Trianon was built by Earl de Grey in 1856 to amuse his grandchildren, and was enjoyed by later generations such as Ettie Fane, later Lady Desborough, Lady Cowper's granddaughter, who lived at Wrest as a child in the 1870s. She recalled it as 'an exquisite little cottage in a shrubbery … It had a delicious smell, all its own, and three tiny rooms, Drawing Room, Dining Room and Kitchen, fitted up with all that the heart of a child could devise for delight.' In front of the Trianon there was formerly a small rock garden, and to the west a hedge concealing it from the dairy.

Left: An early 18th-century Portland stone statue of Atlas holding the globe on his shoulders. It once stood at the centre of the Atlas Pond, which is now filled in

Below left: The Petit Trianon

Below: Interior of the dairy in about 1910 by a local photographer, John Henry Copperwheat, who took many photographs at Wrest in the early 20th century

Henry Earl of Kent Lord Chamberlain to
Maj.ᵗⁱᵉ Queen Anne. A.D. 1705 Ætat 5..

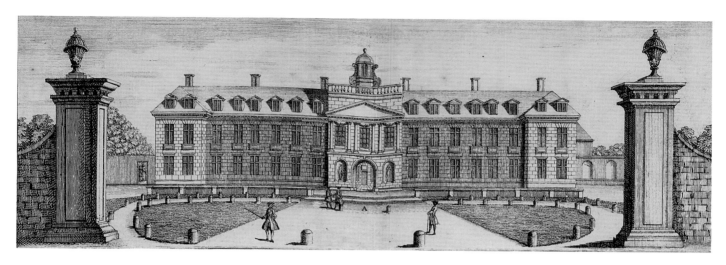

History of Wrest Park

The manor of Wrest is first recorded in the reign of Edward the Confessor (1042–66), when it was held by the thegn, Leofnoth. After the Norman Conquest of 1066 it passed to a man named Hugh as part of the barony of Wahull. The de Greys first settled here in the early 13th century, and Wrest remained their home until the death of Auberon Herbert, 8th Baron Lucas, in 1917.

Three individuals dominated the life of the estate: Henry, Duke of Kent, who laid out the gardens in the early 18th century, continuing the work of his grandmother Amabel and parents, Anthony and Mary; Jemima, Marchioness Grey, who with her husband, Philip Yorke, altered the gardens after 1740; and lastly Thomas, Earl de Grey, who built the current house in the 1830s.

THE EARLY GREYS

The first de Grey to be firmly linked to Wrest is John Grey of Shirland in Derbyshire (c.1205–1266), who acquired a number of manors in Bedfordshire and elsewhere through his marriage to the heiress Emma de Cauz. By the early 14th century the family was established in the county, with the manor at Wrest their principal English residence (they also held Ruthin Castle in Wales).

Family fortunes peaked under Edmund Grey, 4th Baron Grey of Ruthin (1419–90), who was made Lord Treasurer by Edward IV in 1463, and in 1465 created Earl of Kent. On his death his son George inherited about £1,400 – a vast sum at the time. Much of this fortune was squandered by

George's son, the feckless 3rd earl, Richard Grey (1478–1524), who inherited on his father's death in 1503. He sold, mortgaged or gave away most of the family's estates to pay debts from gambling and extravagant living. Wrest and several neighbouring manors were sold to Sir Henry Wyatt in 1512, at prices far below the market value, in Richard's desperation for ready cash. Other of Richard's estates, including nearby Ampthill, were seized by Henry VII, probably in an effort to prevent Richard from destroying his patrimony. By his death in 1524 Richard had confirmed the worst fears of his father that he 'woolde as faste waste & spend hys landes as hys ancestoures purchased them'.

Top: The classical north front of old Wrest house, added in 1672 by Anthony, 11th Earl of Kent, from John Rocque's 1737 plan of Wrest

Above left: The stall plate of Richard, 3rd Earl of Kent, in St George's Chapel, Windsor, dating from c.1505. Richard, as his father had feared, did 'as faste waste & spend hys landes as hys ancestoures purchased them'

Facing page: Henry Grey, Duke of Kent (1671–1740), by Sir Godfrey Kneller, shown with white staff and jewelled key, symbols of his office as Lord Chamberlain

'[John Selden] was solicitor and steward to the Earl of Kent, whose Countess was an ingenious woman … After the earl's death he married her … He never kept any servant peculiar, but my lady's were all at his command'
Speculations of John Aubrey in *Brief Lives*, 1669–96

Above: *Henry Grey, 8th Earl of Kent (c.1583–1639)*
Above right: *Elizabeth Talbot (1581–1651), wife of Henry, 8th Earl of Kent, by the school of Cornelius Janssens*
Right: *The 'Good Countess', Amabel Benn (1607–98), wife of Henry, 10th Earl of Kent, from the school of Sir Peter Lely. Amabel played a central role in managing and developing the estate*

FORTUNES REGAINED

Richard's heir, his half-brother Henry, was able to buy back a few of the Bedfordshire manors, including Wrest, for 450 marks, but could not take up the title of earl due to his modest income. The title remained in abeyance until 1572 when Henry's grandson Reynold was restored to the earldom by Elizabeth I. Family fortunes were restored through the careful stewardship, marriage and position at court of Henry Grey, 6th Earl of Kent (1541–1614), best known for presiding over the trial and execution of Mary, Queen of Scots.

WREST IN THE 17TH CENTURY

The 6th earl was childless, and was succeeded by his brother Charles (d.1623), about whom little is known. Charles's son Henry, the 8th earl (c.1583–1639), married Elizabeth Talbot, who was

renowned as a generous hostess. After Henry's death she stayed on at Wrest with his legal steward, John Selden. The antiquary John Aubrey (1629–97) claimed they had secretly married.

As the 8th earl had no children the title passed to a distant relation, Anthony Grey (1557–1643), a clergyman in his eighties and rector of Aston Flamville in Leicestershire, where he chose to stay, never moving to Wrest. His son, Henry, the 10th earl (1594–1651), was a staunch parliamentarian, and speaker of the House of Lords from 1645 until its temporary abolition in 1649. He married twice: first Mary Courten, whose father, a Flemish refugee, had made his

fortune through trade with Africa and the West Indies; and second Amabel Benn, daughter of the lawyer and judge Sir Anthony Benn.

Amabel, known as the 'Good Countess' for her concern for the poor and her formidable stewardship of the de Grey fortune, outlived Henry by almost 50 years. She played a central role in the development of the estate, together with her son, Anthony (1645–1702), the 11th earl, and his wife, Mary Lucas. Mary inherited a large fortune from her father, Baron Lucas of Shenfield and Crudwell, in 1671, which provided the funds for rebuilding the north front of Wrest house and laying out extensive formal gardens to the south.

THE DUKE OF KENT AND THE 18TH CENTURY

When Anthony, 11th Earl of Kent, collapsed and died on the bowling green at Tunbridge Wells in 1702 his only son, Henry (1671–1740), became 12th Earl of Kent. A cultured man, Henry had developed a keen interest in the arts, architecture and garden design on a Grand Tour of Holland, Germany and Italy during the 1690s. On inheriting Wrest in 1702, he began to improve the gardens to reflect what he had seen on his travels.

To the east of his father's walled garden Henry built two canals, the Mill Pond and the short-lived Mr Ackers's Canal, which was named after the royal gardener Thomas Ackers, who probably had a hand in the design. In 1716 Henry's son Anthony, Earl of Harold (1696–1723), wrote to him from Hanover: 'My sister Bell has amused me very agreeably in one of her last Letters, with an account of sev'ral alterations so much for the better Ye Grace has lately made there, as the filling up of Mr. Ackres cannal, and making a hansome terrass.'

In the park Henry planted avenues imitating the 'delicate walks' he had seen in The Hague and began laying out the great woodland garden to either side of the Long Water.

Henry achieved high office in the court of Queen Anne as a safe pair of hands, his progress deemed the result of political expediency rather than his own ability; he was disliked by many of his contemporaries (who christened him 'Bugg' on

Above: Mary Lucas (d.1702), wife of Anthony, 11th Earl of Kent, by Sir Peter Lely
Left: Portrait of Anthony Grey (1645–1702), 11th Earl of Kent, in 1681, attributed to John Riley
Below: Panoramic view of Wrest gardens from the north, c.1721, attributed to Peter Angelis. Angelis was paid £2 2s. for altering the painting in 1727

Above: Wrest gardens from the south, by Peter Angelis, 1727. The lead statues in the foreground were among those melted down in 1809 by Amabel, Countess de Grey (see page 43)

Right: Henry Grey, Duke of Kent, by George Allen. He wears the badge of the Order of the Garter, to which he was appointed in 1712

account of his pomposity and strong odour). Henry was appointed Lord Chamberlain in 1704, and as such was responsible for organizing royal functions, though he delegated many of his duties.

In 1710 Henry traded in his office of Lord Chamberlain for the title of Duke of Kent. Befitting

his increased status, his work in the gardens at Wrest now aimed to give them greater grandeur. He extended the park to the south and east and removed walls around the 'great parterre', so opening up the view to the Long Water from the house. He added a number of important garden buildings, most notably the baroque pavilion and Cain Hill House (demolished in the 1830s), which were both designed by Thomas Archer and substantially complete by 1711 (see pages 28–30).

Henry continued to revise his garden to keep pace with changes in garden design. In the 1720s and 1730s he introduced newly fashionable informal elements, such as serpentine paths and water features, which were continued by his granddaughter Jemima after 1740. He had also, in 1715, turned his attention to the house, commissioning two plans from the Italian architect Giacomo Leoni, though the scheme was abandoned (see page 22).

Henry was married twice, first to Jemima Crew, with whom he had seven daughters and four sons, and after her death in 1728 to Sophia Bentinck, with whom he had a further two

Left: This 1712 portrait of
Henrietta, Anne and Jane
Grey, daughters of Henry,
Duke of Kent, by George
Allen, shows the pavilion a
year after its completion
Below left: Portraits of the
Duke of Kent's woodcutter
William Millward (left) and
gardener John Duell by
the Anglo-Scottish painter,
Jeremiah Davison
(c.1695–1745). Portraits of
servants from this period are
comparatively rare and
illustrate the esteem in which
the duke must have held his
senior garden staff
Bottom: North-east view of
the Great Garden, by Pieter
Tillemans c.1728, with the
pavilion on the right and
Cain Hill House beyond.
The Obelisk Canal, on the
left, was remodelled as a
sinuous waterway by Batty
Langley in about 1733 and
the obelisk relocated

children. All but two of his 13 children died before
he did, and with no surviving sons he was created
Marquess Grey in May 1740 with the intention that
the title and associated property would pass to his
granddaughter, Jemima Campbell (1723–97). A
few days later, on 22 May 1740, Jemima married
Philip Yorke, son of the Lord Chancellor, the 1st
Earl of Hardwicke.

Within two weeks the old duke was dead and
Jemima inherited Wrest Park and his other estates
(as well as debts of £12,570, which forced her to sell
the family's Herefordshire properties).

JEMIMA, MARCHIONESS GREY

Jemima (1723–97) was born in Copenhagen, where her father was envoy to the Danish court. In 1725 she moved with her mother, Amabel, and brother to live with her maternal grandparents at Wrest. She remained with them on her mother's early death but after her grandfather the duke remarried in 1729 she went to live in Chelsea with her aunt Mary Grey (only three years her senior) under the watchful eye of Thomas Secker, rector of St James's, Piccadilly. Through Secker she met Catherine Talbot, a child prodigy, who became a lifelong friend, and encouraged Jemima's love of books and intellectual pursuits.

Her marriage to Philip Yorke was a great success, and in 50 years together they were only apart for any significant period once, in 1749. Jemima left estate management to Philip and his father, Lord Chancellor Hardwicke, but showed a keen interest in the gardens, which she had enjoyed in her youth both as a peaceful retreat and a place in which to entertain. Her affection for Wrest is clear from her many letters written while staying here during the summer months; she wrote to her daughter Amabel: 'I don't wonder you should suspect that the finer Places I have seen should make Wrest appear less Delightful to me – but my Dear, home has always beauties … that no other place can equal.' In 1745 Catherine Talbot described Jemima's daily routine, which consisted of morning prayers, a walk in the park, tea in the garden buildings or, if the weather did not permit it, chess or billiards in the house. In the evenings there was an hour of scholarly reading. After a visit of Philip's parents, Lord and Lady Hardwicke, Philip's sister Elizabeth wrote: 'Papa has said so much at dinner today of Wrest, of the improvements made in the house, of the beauty of the garden, the excellence of the pineapples, cherries, strawberries, venison, etc., etc., and above all the company, that I can form no idea how it is possible to live anywhere else.'

The young Jemima, although keen to improve her inheritance, made only limited alterations to the Great Garden, with the advice of her tutor Thomas Wright, and later of 'Capability' Brown (see page 15). At Wimpole, which she and Philip inherited from Lord Hardwicke in 1764, they allowed Brown more of a free rein, but at Wrest she wanted to preserve the 'Mystery of the Gardens' for future generations.

'I have been to the Wedgewoods exhibition of his service for the Czarina, & want very much to have some of our views of your drawing find a place in it, as it is not quite compleated. How can they be got at? Have you any book that contains them at Wrest or are they in your great book locked up in London? If so could you send me the key – and another question, should you care to send out any drawings not framed? I believe they were all fixed. Those I should wish for are … the different views of the water round the garden at Wrest … also the Bath & Room at Wrest which you took lately if that too could be finished up. These smaller views I suppose you have with you, but if they cannot be taken out or would not be safe to send up & lend out, I by no means wish to hazard them.'
Jemima, writing to her daughter Amabel, Lady Polwarth, on 19 January 1774

AMABEL, COUNTESS DE GREY

After Jemima's death in 1797 Wrest passed to her daughter Amabel (1751–1833) who shared her love of reading, politics and the arts. Amabel's meticulously kept journal gives a vivid insight into life at Wrest from the 1760s until shortly before her death in 1833. She was already widowed when she inherited the estate. Her husband, Alexander Hume-Campbell, Lord Polwarth, died at the age of 31 of consumption, and was mourned by Amabel in her diary as 'the friend & protector I had hoped for'. He had been a keen agricultural improver and set up a model farm at Clophill. He also established a pack of hounds at Wrest, much to Philip and Jemima's distaste.

Amabel was an accomplished artist; eight of her views of Wimpole Hall (inherited by her father in 1764) and Wrest were used on Wedgwood's Green Frog dinner service presented to Catherine the Great of Russia in 1774. During her tenure much of the estate was enclosed, allowing farms to be consolidated. Parts of the park were also let for grazing, and many of the duke's lead statues were melted down to provide lead for repairing the roof of the house. Amabel later recalled this with regret as seeming to depopulate the gardens.

Her journals reveal less of an emotional attachment to Wrest than her mother had. There are none of the frequent observations on the atmosphere of the gardens that occur in Jemima's letters. Instead, Amabel dwells on the economic difficulties of managing the vast estate. Soon after inheriting, in 1797, she wrote, 'I have an Estate & Country Seat whose Idea was always pleasant to me from my Childhood, & yet I fear I shall be harrass'd with the Trouble & Expense they bring.'

During her later years her young nephew Thomas Robinson, 3rd Baron Grantham and later 2nd Earl de Grey, took an increasing interest in Wrest. The French-style entrance lodges he erected flanking the Silsoe gate in 1826 match the style he later used when rebuilding the house. The impressive new Silsoe gate and drive also emphasized that this western approach was now the main entrance to the park. Thomas was already forming ideas for the main house: 'they looked so well and appropriate when finished that I felt quite confirmed as to the taste and the style of architecture, if ever I built a new house.'

Left: The Silsoe gate and lodges in a photograph of the 1930s. They were designed by Thomas Robinson (later 2nd Earl de Grey), in his first use of the French style, in 1826, before he inherited the estate from his aunt Amabel

The de Grey Mausoleum

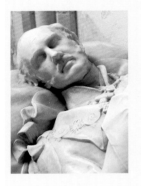

The mausoleum contains one of the greatest collections of funerary monuments in England, dating from the 16th to the 19th centuries

Two miles west of Wrest Park in Flitton village lies the church of St John the Baptist, built by the de Greys in the mid 15th century. Attached to it is the remarkable de Grey family mausoleum that holds one of the greatest collections of funerary monuments in England, dating from the 16th to the 19th centuries, and ranging in style from late Gothic, Jacobean, baroque and neoclassical to the neo-Gothic.

The mausoleum originated in the 'little Chappell or buryall place' built by Henry Grey, 6th Earl of Kent shortly before his death in 1614. In the early 18th century Henry, Duke of Kent added to this simple chamber arms to the north, south and east, and a central crossing chamber to create the distinctive cruciform plan. Further alterations were made to accommodate the tomb of Thomas, Earl de Grey, the last of the family buried here, in 1859.

The earliest monument in the mausoleum is that of its founder, Henry, 6th Earl of Kent, in richly coloured alabaster; the finest is undoubtedly John Michael Rysbrack's effigy of Henry, Duke of Kent, and his two wives, against the north wall of the east chamber. His children, all but two of whom died before him, are commemorated in the central and northern chambers. The only neoclassical monument is that

of Philip Yorke, husband of Jemima and 2nd Earl of Hardwicke, now flanked by memorials to his two daughters and placed opposite the duke's effigy.

The fine monuments to the 2nd Earl de Grey and his wife, Henrietta (d.1848), that conclude the series are quite different in style. The former rests on a neo-Gothic chest tomb, a conventional style for the tombs of noblemen in the later 19th century. The classical monument by the Irish sculptor Terence Farrell to Henrietta is a moving tableau showing the family grieving at her coffin while an angel escorts her soul to heaven above – a vivid display of Victorian piety and loss.

EARL DE GREY, AND THE NEW HOUSE

Thomas Philip Robinson (1781–1859) was born in London to Thomas Robinson, 2nd Baron Grantham, and Mary Jemima Yorke, younger daughter of Jemima, Marchioness Grey. During his long life he bore three names: Robinson, Weddell (a condition of the inheritance of a distant cousin's estate) and, from 1833, de Grey, on inheriting that title and the lands at Wrest. In 1805 he married Henrietta Frances Cole, fifth daughter of the Earl of Enniskillen, and they had five children, though only two daughters survived them.

By the time he died in 1859 de Grey had made small but vital differences in the fields of his many interests, notably in architecture (see page 11). He was keen on the new sport of yachting, and built a house at Cowes as a result. He was committed to the Yeomanry, particularly the Yorkshire Hussars, of which he was commanding officer for many years, and was a fellow of the Royal Society and of the Society of Antiquaries. He was also, from 1818 until his death, Lord Lieutenant of Bedfordshire.

Although de Grey preferred 'to move among men of letters and artists' his responsibilities as a peer and one of the richest landowners in England he took seriously and was involved in politics. He became First Lord of the Admiralty in 1834. His brother, Viscount Goderich, was for a brief period the prime minister, and de Grey served reluctantly as Lord Lieutenant of Ireland from 1841 to 1844.

'Without vanity I may say that there are very few things of which I do not know something. I am afraid that the phrase "Jack of all trades and master of none" may apply; but the general liking and wish to know, and indeed to practise, many different trades, has been a source of much pleasure to me all my life.'

From the memoirs of Earl de Grey (left, c.1827, when still Lord Grantham, by John Wood, who painted the ceilings in the library and drawing room, after William Robinson)

Although it was not uncommon for an aristocrat to have wide-ranging interests, de Grey was unusually committed to his. He may have deemed himself to be 'Jack of all trades and master of none' (see box), but there were some areas of his life, notably architecture, in which he can be considered expert, as Wrest house demonstrates.

Below left: *The conservatory and Italian Garden in Earl de Grey's sketchbook, 'Views of Wrest', 1831. The garden layout shown is probably a proposal as it differs markedly from later illustrations*

Above: *Sketch of about 1826 by de Grey's youngest child, Amabel Elizabeth, entitled 'My Papa Lord Grantham by his daughter Amabel Robinson.' She died a year later, aged 11*

De Grey Family Tree

Successive ownership of Wrest Park is shown in red

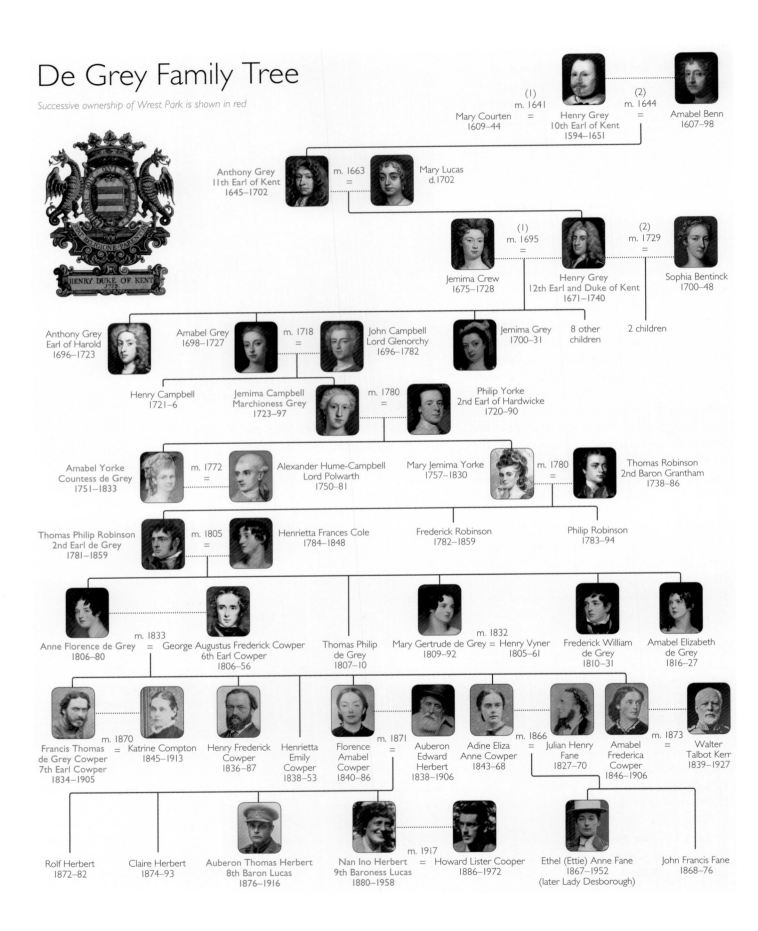

(1)
m. 1641
Mary Courten
1609–44
=
Henry Grey
10th Earl of Kent
1594–1651
(2)
m. 1644
=
Amabel Benn
1607–98

Anthony Grey
11th Earl of Kent
1645–1702
m. 1663
=
Mary Lucas
d.1702

Jemima Crew
1675–1728
(1)
m. 1695
=
Henry Grey
12th Earl and Duke of Kent
1671–1740
(2)
m. 1729
=
Sophia Bentinck
1700–48

Anthony Grey
Earl of Harold
1696–1723

Amabel Grey
1698–1727
m. 1718
=
John Campbell
Lord Glenorchy
1696–1782

Jemima Grey
1700–31

8 other
children

2 children

Henry Campbell
1721–6

Jemima Campbell
Marchioness Grey
1723–97
m. 1780
=
Philip Yorke
2nd Earl of Hardwicke
1720–90

Amabel Yorke
Countess de Grey
1751–1833
m. 1772
=
Alexander Hume-Campbell
Lord Polwarth
1750–81

Mary Jemima Yorke
1757–1830
m. 1780
=
Thomas Robinson
2nd Baron Grantham
1738–86

Thomas Philip Robinson
2nd Earl de Grey
1781–1859
m. 1805
=
Henrietta Frances Cole
1784–1848

Frederick Robinson
1782–1859

Philip Robinson
1783–94

Anne Florence de Grey
1806–80
=
George Augustus Frederick Cowper
6th Earl Cowper
1806–56
m. 1833

Thomas Philip
de Grey
1807–10

Mary Gertrude de Grey
1809–92
=
Henry Vyner
1805–61
m. 1832

Frederick William
de Grey
1810–31

Amabel Elizabeth
de Grey
1816–27

Francis Thomas
de Grey Cowper
7th Earl Cowper
1834–1905
m. 1870
=
Katrine Compton
1845–1913

Henry Frederick
Cowper
1836–87

Henrietta
Emily
Cowper
1838–53

Florence
Amabel
Cowper
1840–86
m. 1871
=
Auberon
Edward
Herbert
1838–1906

Adine Eliza
Anne Cowper
1843–68
m. 1866
=
Julian Henry
Fane
1827–70

Amabel
Frederica
Cowper
1846–1906
m. 1873
=
Walter
Talbot Kerr
1839–1927

Rolf Herbert
1872–82

Claire Herbert
1874–93

Auberon Thomas Herbert
8th Baron Lucas
1876–1916

Nan Ino Herbert
9th Baroness Lucas
1880–1958
m. 1917
=
Howard Lister Cooper
1886–1972

Ethel (Ettie) Anne Fane
1867–1952
(later Lady Desborough)

John Francis Fane
1868–76

HENRY DUKE OF KENT
1713

LAST OF THE DE GREYS AT WREST

After Earl de Grey's death in 1859 Wrest Park passed to his daughter Anne (1806–80), whose husband, the 6th Earl Cowper, had died in 1856. Anne, a staunch evangelical, gave generous support to local charities and village institutions. She made few changes to the house or grounds, but saw that they were well maintained. One of her daughters, Adine, died in 1868, and when Adine's husband also died, in 1870, Anne took in their two small children: John (who died six years later) and Ethel (Ettie). That same year Anne's eldest son, Francis (1834–1905), now 7th Earl Cowper, married Katrine Compton, daughter of the Marquess of Northampton.

Anne died in 1880. Her estates were inherited by Francis, a Whig grandee and already extremely rich. He divided his time between his main seat at Panshanger in Hertfordshire, his London house, and his shooting estates in Scotland, visiting Wrest only occasionally for country-house parties. He and Katrine had no children of their own (although the marriage was a success) and virtually adopted Ettie. They were members of the aristocratic circle known as the Souls, who objected to what they deemed the cultural and intellectual indifference of their society, cultivating close friendships based on conversation and shared ideas.

When Francis died in 1905 his estates were divided; he left Panshanger to Ettie and Wrest and the title of Baron Lucas to Auberon Herbert (1876–1916), son of his sister Florence. The 8th baron, known as Bron, was a keen sportsman, despite losing a leg while a correspondent for *The*

Times during the Boer War. He preferred to live at Picket Post in the New Forest, and leased out Wrest Park from 1906 to 1912 to the American ambassador, Whitelaw Reid, who described the gardens in a letter to his father-in-law in September 1905 as 'the finest private grounds I have yet seen in England' with 'magnificent woods' and 'a sort of temple … with a big dome, used occasionally for a picnic dinner and regularly for the lunches during the shooting season'.

Bron served in the Liberal government from 1908, rising to the position of president of the Board of Agriculture and Fisheries in 1914, but left politics a year later to join the Royal Flying Corps despite being substantially over-age.

Life at Wrest

An endearing account of Wrest comes from the memoirs of Ettie Fane (1867–1952), one of the granddaughters of Lady Anne Cowper and the 6th earl, who lived here as a child in the 1870s after the early death of both her parents. One winter she and her cousins 'all learnt to skate, and fell about very happily on the Pavilion pond'. Of arrangements inside the house Ettie recalled: 'There was only one bathroom in that lovely house, and I never knew it used. Our nurseries were at the top of the house, and our nursery maids staggered up the vast stone stairs four times a day, carrying heavy trays of meals. The downstairs rooms were lit by lamps, wheeled round the house on trolleys, but in the upstairs rooms there were only candles – few and far between.'

Left: Ettie Fane, by then Lady Desborough, in July 1888; detail of a photograph pasted in the Wrest Park and Panshanger visitor book

Top: House party at Wrest in August 1888. The group is posed on the steps in front of the conservatory. Standing at the centre back is Francis, 7th Earl Cowper. His wife, Katrine, is seated immediately in front of him, wearing a pale hat with a black band

Above: Bron Herbert in his uniform as officer in the Royal Flying Corps in the spring of 1916. He was killed flying over German lines that November

Wrest Park: A First World War Hospital

Wrest Park was almost certainly the first country house to take in wounded soldiers during the First World War. It opened to patients on 7 September 1914, just two weeks after the first major engagement of British troops at the Battle of Mons.

Initially Wrest was used as a convalescent home, providing somewhere for soldiers to recuperate after being discharged from hospital. It was the first of many grand houses to be used in this way. By the end of the war there were 1,484 auxiliary hospitals (offering 84,689 beds) across the country, and an even larger number of convalescent homes. Both played a vital role in the war effort, providing the extra capacity that was sorely needed to cope with the mass casualties of trench warfare.

Bron, Lord Lucas, was kept busy in London as a government minister, so it was his sister, Nan, who supervised the running of the hospital. Bron wrote on 8 September to their cousin Ettie Desborough: '66 convalescents, the very first, I believe, to leave hospital, went down to Wrest yesterday. Nan heard late on Saturday night that they were coming, but they just managed to get everything ready in time, and she says that it is all going very well, and the men are extremely happy and very jolly.' Nan's diary gives a detailed picture of life at Wrest at the time. Early

entries depict an atmosphere somewhat like a holiday camp: the men went boating on the lakes in the grounds, fished, played cricket and football, dressed up and put on theatricals in the staircase hall and went on regular outings.

In October 1914 Wrest convalescent home was briefly closed when the last of the 66 convalescents returned to duty. It reopened a month later as a base hospital, run jointly with nearby Woburn Abbey, receiving wounded soldiers directly from the front. The first 100 patients arrived on 20 November, brought by ambulance from Ampthill station. Conversion from convalescent home to hospital had been achieved in little more than a week.

The ground-floor reception rooms became A-Ward, taking the most serious cases. B-Ward was in the large first-floor bedrooms on the south side of the house, and C-Ward was hidden away in the bachelors' wing (a section of the service wing). The medical officer, X-ray equipment and operating theatre occupied rooms on the north side of the first floor, and a Stripping Room (for delousing the soldiers) was set up off the stable yard. The 24 nurses were accommodated in the servants' bedrooms on the second floor.

In February 1915, following an intensive course of training at the Metropolitan Hospital, Nan took over as matron from the ineffectual Sister Martin. For the next two years she ran the hospital with military precision. Officially Wrest had 150 beds, though on occasion there were 200 patients in residence. Once well enough, the soldiers were moved on to a ring of convalescent homes set up nearby, freeing up space for new arrivals. In all, 1,600 men passed through the hospital's wards. By 1916 it had a deserved reputation as the best country house base hospital.

Top left: A convalescent soldier after a successful fishing trip at Wrest, 1914
Top middle: Convalescents and a nurse beside Old Park Water (the western encircling canal) in 1914
Top right: Wrest Park hospital ambulances outside the stable block in 1915
Above: Nurse feeding the pet swan named the 'Probationer' in the autumn of 1914. There were 24 nurses to tend about 130 patients at the time
Left: The library as A-Ward IV in November 1914. Note the temporary electric lighting and screens covering the ornate bookcases

Top: Aftermath of the fire in 1916. The patients and staff were evacuated and most of the furniture saved
Above: Hospital bedding piled up in the staircase hall following the fire of 1916
Right: Mr and Mrs Murray (foreground) at Wrest during a shoot, 24 November 1923
Below: Guests in the entrance hall at Wrest for the Oakley Hunt Ball, which Murray hosted on several occasions in the 1920s

PERIOD OF DECLINE

When war broke out in July 1914 Bron offered Wrest to the Admiralty for use as a hospital. The house was readied for the purpose, as reported by a local newspaper: 'All the portable furniture in the dining and drawing room and the library has been removed and over 100 beds erected while the bedrooms have been given up to nursing staff, and the electric light is being temporarily installed.'

In the event, the Navy had no use for it, so Wrest served as a convalescent home for soldiers until November 1914, when rising war casualties meant that it became a hospital. Bron's sister, Nan, served as matron and the wounded were received from the front by train (see pages 48–9). The hospital closed in September 1916 after the house

was badly damaged by fire. Repairs were soon made, but plans were already in place for its sale when Bron was killed in action that November.

JOHN GEORGE MURRAY

In September 1917 John George Murray (1865–1954), a brewing and mining magnate from Consett, County Durham, bought Wrest. Though viewed with suspicion by the villagers, Murray made efforts to embed himself in Bedfordshire society: he became a magistrate, was elected Chairman of the Bedfordshire Chamber of Agriculture in 1921 and 1922, and set up a private hunting pack, the Wrest Basset Hounds. He made substantial repairs to the house, redecorated bedrooms, introduced electric lighting, and made changes to the gardens, mostly to make them easier to manage.

Both the Rose Garden and Italian Garden Murray replanted with simpler displays of annuals, and the Evergreen Garden was replaced by four Atlas Cedars. Many of the statues were repositioned. The further reaches of the garden were, however, neglected and in 1925 the grounds were described as 'too big and not kept up well'.

By the early 1930s Murray's attentions were diverted elsewhere as he embarked on a series of acquisitions to expand his brewing business in the north-east. In 1932 he moved to the more modest Coles Park in Hertfordshire and put Wrest up for sale. Unable to sell quickly Murray began asset stripping the estate to raise funds. Many of the

trees in the park were felled by the Essex Timber Company and a number of the garden ornaments were sold or moved to Coles Park; some, including a pair of cast iron wyverns, were sold back to Nan Herbert, Lady Lucas, whose agent visited the by now neglected estate in 1935.

THE SECOND WORLD WAR
The Sun Insurance Company
The house and about 260 acres (105ha) of the park were eventually bought in June 1939 by the Sun Insurance Company for use as their wartime headquarters. The rest of the land was sold and incorporated into neighbouring farms, and the furniture auctioned off from a marquee on the lawn. The portraits in the staircase hall were bought by the company and so remained at Wrest.

During the war over 300 Sun Insurance employees were based at Wrest, many living on site. To accommodate them the stable block was converted into dormitories and a number of timber dormitory huts were built to the south of the service wing. Most of the rooms in the house were used as offices, though the ante-library was reserved for recreation. There were dances and occasional concerts or theatricals in the staircase hall, and staff would gather here daily to listen to the one o'clock news. In the grounds they played tennis, cricket and football, and went boating on the lakes. Though volunteers maintained some of the gardens close to the house, the grounds were generally neglected and much of the parkland was ploughed up to help the war effort.

The Silsoe Institute
In 1946 Wrest Park was bought by the Ministry of Works, and soon after leased to the National Institute of Agricultural Engineering (later the Silsoe Research Institute), which was responsible for maintaining the gardens. The garden buildings and statuary remained in the care of the Ministry, which opened the grounds to visitors under supervision. The parkland beyond the garden was used for agriculture, offices and laboratories were added to the east and north-east of the house, and new glasshouses and plant-growing areas were established in the walled garden. Earl de Grey's library became the Institute library, and the drawing room and Countess's Sitting Room were used for meetings and conferences.

Sun Insurance and the Home Guard
Peter and Eunice Hoare met at Wrest when working for Sun Insurance during the Second World War. Eunice slept in the converted stable block with eight other women, including her sister, before moving to the new huts south of the dairy, which she much preferred: 'You had your own little cubicle'. Peter remembers his weekly drill, as part of the Home Guard, and fire-watching duty on the roof. He left Wrest in August 1942 to join the RAF, but Eunice remained until the end of the war. They married in 1945.

Top: Sun Insurance staff on the terrace steps in the 1940s
Below left: Peter Hoare in front of one of the dormitory huts south of the dairy

Above: Peter Hoare on manoeuvres with the Wrest Park Home Guard, July 1941
Below: Eunice Miatt (far left), with girls from her dormitory

'We had a chicken picker … It would go into a darkened shed … and sweep them up ever so gently. We had a stand up at the Royal Show and we took it there and put balloons in it to show that it didn't hurt the chickens.' Alan Hunter (below, at Wrest), recalling a Silsoe Institute invention

Top: Grounds below the round pond being ploughed in about 1959. By 1960 the area was in use by the Silsoe Institute for potato experiments
Below: The Long Water today

For over 80 years the Institute was the main centre for agricultural engineering research in the country and built up an international reputation. Scientists working here researched farm mechanization, food processing and environmental management, and ran trials on new techniques and equipment. Edwina Holden, a typist and later a secretary for the Institute, and Alan Hunter, a technician in the greenhouses put up in the kitchen garden, recall the many dignitaries who came to view the facilities, including the Duke of Edinburgh and the Prince of Wales, and the machinery invented at Wrest. This included a milking robot, blackcurrant harvester, mushroom picker, which 'would only pick out the right size', and 'an overhead carrying system for bananas' to reduce crop damage during transit in the West Indies.

The social life of the Institute centred on the Social Club based in the extended dairy. It organized dances, sports events and the yearly raft race on the Long Water.

WREST TODAY

Since 1947 many of the garden buildings and ornaments have been repaired and conserved by the Ministry of Works and more recently English Heritage. The conservation of the gardens, however, was initially rather ad hoc, with some non-historic planting, and in 1981 the A6 was diverted through the parkland, separating the Silsoe gate lodges from their historic context. The first detailed plan for restoration of the gardens appeared in 1983, and since then much work has been carried out to restore the Great Garden to its 18th-century glory.

In 2006 the Silsoe Institute closed. English Heritage took over the house and eastern service buildings and is working on a 20-year plan to restore the gardens to their appearance before the estate was sold in 1917. In 2014 the Wrest Park Collections store opened in the former Silsoe Institute buildings off the stable yard, and can be viewed by appointment. It holds over 153,000 artefacts from sites within English Heritage's care, spanning 2,000 years, from prehistoric antlers and Roman masonry to Victorian banisters.